Drum

Twisters:

The

Book

That

Will

Make

You

Smile

With ...

Frustration!

A Big "Cheers" Goes Out To:

Shelly Heidel, Heidi, Tazo, Gary Evans, Tetley, Sean Rogers, JoJo Mayer, The Mayor, Lipton, Kian Blewett, Lisa DeBeer, beer, Batman (spoiler alert: aka Bruce Wayne), Johnny Rabb, Bugs Bunny, Typhoo, Scott Sanders, Colonel Sanders, Twinings, Coke (a Cola), Andy Ziker, my family, Apple Inc., Orange Inc., lemons, the Mighty Leaf, Ydna Murd, the Count, bear traps, PG Tips, a bloke I met yesterday on the train, Dan Britt (for the YMCA joke), Yorkshire Tea, Bill Ray, Cyrus, Vic Firth, Colin Firth, Harney & Sons, Bill Bachman, Turner, Overdrive, Greedo (the one who shot first), Barry's, me, myself, I, and most importantly ... Gloria Estefan!

All illustrations by Alan Schulz, Atlanta

Contents

How Am I Supposed To Use This Book?

First, you grab the corner of the page with your thumb and forefinger and then casually turn the page over ... (People viewing on e-readers need to consult with the instructions of said e-reader, preferably in their own language, or it will make less sense than it does already.)

Now that you have that down, let's discuss what this book is all about. If you've gone ahead and sneaked a quick peek through all of this gobbledygook, then you are probably feeling a little stumped. No, this is not your ordinary, run-of-the-(tread)mill type of publication, because you will actually be *getting somewhere* (cue smirk). Please don't treat the material here like you would a method book or something that you should be tackling first before anything else. If you wish to learn how to play the drums the conventional way, then may I kindly recommend my own series of method books, the rather exquisite *The Teacher and Student Method Drum Set Studies: Exercise Books One & Two.* Jolly good, sport!

What we are doing here is going against the grain. Getting rebellious. Causing a stir. Going a little potty. Taking a leap of faith. Having a giraffe. Being pretentious (French). Talking about a revolution. Okay, you get the picture now. The exercises here should be approached like small but fascinating puzzles that will captivate your heart but boggle your mind. You should go ahead and learn what you need to learn with your instructional books (or videos), and then have a dainty stroll over here afterwards to, as Apple would say, "Think Different."

Confused still? Well, think of your method books as being the angel on one shoulder, and us being El Diablo on the other. Or, if that's not your thing, consider the others to be the Jedi Masters and us the Sith Lords (but The Force *is* still strong here). However, we're not trying to *un*-teach you everything that you have been taught. Instead we offer your programming a bit of a reboot so you are not just following what everyone else is doing. After all, we don't want to keep creating the same old "drum machines" time after time, do we now?

Consider the exercises in this book as blueprints. Get the basics down first, and then feel free to interpret it all your own way, depending on your skill level and tastes. For example, if you are the groovy kind, then funk it up by "ghosting" all of the snares that are "off" the beat. This will add a little color. Also, try playing the exercises faster each time until you have reached your own personal speed limit. This will give you a workout and challenge you even further.

When all is said and done, try to make these beats your own. I promise not to sue you!

Whose (Drum) Twisted Mind Did I Just Enter?

Yes, that'll be mine. My name is Owen Liversidge, and I am an Englishman that crossed the pond to live in the United States. You could possibly consider me as being a "fish out of water," but I think of my situation more as "fish and chips out of the newspaper." (Plates are far too civilized.) Either way, just try to bear with me as I will do my very best to string you along without tying you in too many knots. Alas, I can make you no promises though, my dear friends!

So, anyway, the language here may be a bit mixed. My humor is still one of insatiable British wit, but I spell things the "American English" way (Don't you just love that term?) I blame my computer because I bought it in the US and it keeps on correcting me. Please get over it, because I cannot be bothered to create an "English" and "US" version of this book. You say "po-tay-to," I say "po-tah-to," but let's not call the whole thing off, okay? And to anyone reading this from a country other than the UK and the USA ... I'm sorry! (Except if you're a Canadian, that is.)

Admittedly, I do possess some of the English stereotypes. My skin is whiter than an albino polar bear's arse [sic], and I drink lots of tea. With milk. Because that's normal. Remember that! However, I also visit the dentist regularly, so my talking like a pirate is not matched with looking like one. Other than that, I like to be literal, and so consider "football" to be something that you *use your feet with which to move a ball around.* (I always get a "kick" out of that one.) Chuckle.

So then, my fellow brothers and sisters (and Mormons), let's delve into the brave new world of *Drum Twisters: The Book That Will Make You Smile With ... Frustration!* Follow me along these pages (or pixels) of stuff that your mother only warned you about. We shall be taking a journey into the unknown, rife with both torment and merriment. You will be able to play things that you never even knew were possible, as well as learning that there are many different substitutions for the word "look." Also, your tastebuds will probably feel the desire to drink more tea, but don't blame me, because I am just helping you to realize what has been missing from your life (other than playing the drums).

Okay, enough of this drivel now. Let's get started. As the book title suggests, just remember that you will get frustrated from time to time, so never forget to smile along the way ...

H a p p y   d r u m m i n g !

And

So

It

All

Begins ...

Chapter One: What's All This "Backbeat" Nonsense About Then?

First things first! Before learning how to turn the beat around (and upside down), we must come to an understanding. Let us begin by establishing exactly what a "backbeat" is. The backbeat is what we perceive as being the *sharp rhythmic accent of a beat or measure*. Some like to call it the "pulse" of the music. As drummers, this is where we usually place our good old snare hits, as they stand out and generally remain more consistent than the kicks. Up until now, you've mostly been hitting the snare continuously on the "2" and the "4," as this pattern dominates the styles of rock and pop music, as well as mainstream jazz. It can be known as *the* backbeat, although the cooler ones among us like to think of it as "playing in the pocket." It's the key component that keeps a piece of music grounded and flowing merrily along. It's also what gets your booty moving, hips gyrating (oo-er), feet tapping, heads bopping and even your granny up on the dancefloor. The listeners and players can establish a steady motion behind the music and therefore "move" along with it, whatever that movement may be. (Get your mind out of the gutter!) It's all about going with the flow, or flowing with the go.

Of course, there are other styles of music that approach things a little differently, and we will be getting into some of those later. For now, though, we're going to examine the most common positioning of our backbeats, chop it all up, and then paste it back together again.

Getting off the beat(en) path ...

Let's now take a quick and simple look at what we are talking about here, within the context of a straightforward eighth note beat (the ones that you have played more times than you've taken breaths). You will notice that the snare strikes are on the "2" and the "4," making them the backbeats for this demonstration. Take note of the accents as denoting our backbeats:

Now that we have established what the regular backbeats actually are, we should next entertain the idea of throwing convention out of the window ... kersplat! Or, as Master Yoda would say, "You must unlearn what you have learned!" In other words, let's step outside of our comfort zones and mix things up a little.

The options we have are to move either just one or both of our backbeats. In the following examples, let's start by simply moving the second backbeat (the "4") to all other available locations after the first backbeat (the "2"). To keep things straightforward, we're still going to refer to them as "backbeats." They also remain accented:

Now, let's do the same thing with the first backbeat (the "2") by moving it to all other available locations before the second backbeat (the "4"):

Finally, let's get all crazy inside and try moving both of them around a bit. This might require you to go and lie down awhile afterwards:

I know, I know ... I was sneaky and put in an extra backbeat on those last two exercises for you! This is simply to illustrate the fact there we are not stuck with just two backbeats and we can create several, if we so please. It's all about how we want the pulse to flow (or not, as the case may be) by establishing our "hits" within the movement of the music.

Our friends in Latin America already understand this pretty well. If you ever listen to a bossa nova, mambo, or a rumba, for example, you will hear that the accented hits are not on the "2" and the "4" exclusively. This is because the señors playing on the drum set are following what is known as a "clave" pattern or rhythm, used in Afro-Cuban music. Traditionally, the clave player in a percussion ensemble would be the main timekeeper and rhythmist, keeping everything together by providing a pattern or template for the others to follow. Yes, drummers come from quite a sophisticated background you know ... belch! Excuse me.

The best-known clave rhythms are the 3/2 and 2/3 patterns. By following a two measure framework, you simply place two hits in one bar and three in the other. Here is a look at how some of those patterns work, so try to clap out the following (similar) rhythms:

We're exploring clave patterns because it's important to understand that we're not treading on any new ground here. Popular music in the western hemisphere has (purposefully) created a safe and easily accessible format, which the listener feels a quick connection with. That's why most pop "walks" along with a steady stride, so that we feel like we can all "walk" along with it ... gosh, that was a fabulous metaphor, even if I do say so myself!

However, music from other parts of the world often "walks" off the beat(en) path, such as with these Afro-Cuban clave patterns. Let us now try placing all of those previous patterns within the context of a steady eighth note hi-hat rhythm:

2 / 3 SON CLAVE:

3 / 2 SON CLAVE:

2 / 3 RUMBA CLAVE:

3 / 2 RUMBA CLAVE:

Okay then, I sense that you are all starting to get itchy feet. Of course, we don't want our snare hits to get lonely, so we can now start to think about adding in some kick drum. Steady on there, old bean ... let's ease into this gently now! We're not going to try and perform some full Latin beats just yet, we should get used to some straightforward quarter note counts first. For the son clave beats, we will add in the kick drum for the quarter counts (1, 2, 3, 4) where there are no snare hits. Then, for the rumba clave, we will just go ahead and use straight quarter counts on the kick, no matter what else is going on.

Sound like a plan? Lovely then, here we go:

Almost there, now ... I've got one more exercise for you, though. We need to look at our Latin kick pattern first by itself. Try out this repetitive rhythm on your kick drum:

Sorted! Let's now add that kick pattern to our clave rhythms to finish it all up:

2 / 3 SON CLAVE:

3 / 2 SON CLAVE:

2 / 3 RUMBA CLAVE:

3 / 2 RUMBA CLAVE:

It was all lies, I tell you, because there is still one more! We will now round off this look at Afro-Cuban clave patterns by examining the bossa nova. This is probably the most well-known of all Latin beats, so I guess we've gone and saved the best for last:

2 / 3 BOSSA NOVA CLAVE:

3 / 2 BOSSA NOVA CLAVE:

Right, that's it. I promise you, this time! (Scout's honor.)

Of course, there are many more Latin beats out there, but we've looked at the most popular that commonly use an eighth note hi-hat pattern. These beats are not confined to South America either because many jazz legends have used clave rhythms and made them their own. If you are wondering what I am talking about, then you should seriously check out the likes of Gene Krupa, Max Roach, Cozy Cole, and of course, Buddy Rich.

The most important thing to ponder over now, though, is what are YOU going to do with these concepts?

Chapter Two: Are You Down For The Count?

In our quest to move away from the conventional, we will take a much broader look at eighth note beats with differing backbeats. Another way to look at these patterns is to consider the use of "snare displacements," because we are *dis*-placing them from the norm (or whatever he is called). Of course, we are talking about displacement in a purposeful manner here, not the same as when you lose your cup of Earl Grey or even your marbles. Every now and again, these beats find their way into mainstream music. Think of "Beautiful Day" by U2, or "Clocks" by Coldplay as some more recent examples. A lot of the time, these beats are considered to be short snippets of "polyrhythms." No, a polyrhythm is not a drumming parrot, but a piece of music where two contrasting rhythms (or beats) occur at the same time. It's kind of like the dichotomy of music. Are you wondering what the heck I am talking about? Well, let's look once again at our bossa nova beat as an example:

Now, take a close look at the kick drum pattern at the bottom. As you can see, it is following an ostinato pattern of one "on" then two "off" then one "on," with regard to following the eighth notes; it follows a steady, repeating framework of FOUR notes at a time: 1, (2), (3), 4, which continues on throughout the repeats. Our snare drum is following a two "off" and one "on" pattern, which is a repeating framework of THREE notes at a time: (1), (2), 3. And, as the exercise contains sixteen counts of eighth notes in total (8+8), we cannot consistently carry the snare pattern on into the repeats because three won't go evenly into sixteen. So, we have a spare (1) at the end. Confused? So am I! (It's all about those darn number crunches.)

As the pattern of THREE (on snare) is directly above the pattern of FOUR (on kick), we refer to this polyrhythm as a "THREE to FOUR" pattern. Others might call it a "THREE over FOUR" or "THREE against FOUR" pattern. (I, however, am a pacifist, so I'm not "against" anything, except the back of my sofa.)

Here are some additional eighth note beats for the three to four (3:4) polyrhythmic pattern, with the same kick as before but using the other snare hits in our pattern of three:

To give these beats more of a rock edge and allow them to "drive" along, we can simply keep the eighth notes flowing by using the kick with ALL of the hi-hats in between the snares. Let's look again at those bossa nova variations, now with a steady eighth note rhythm below:

The odd measure on that last group of exercises may look familiar. Some modern contemporary styles of rock and pop like to use snare displacement but manage to achieve a more flowing pattern by never letting up on the constant eighth note rhythm ... it's all about pound-for-pound and pounding it away! However, I know that all of you are (still) here because, like me, you have been searching for the meaning in Gloria Estefan's words. So then, we shall get back on (or off) track, and take a quick gander at some additional polyrhythms that use an eighth note hi-hat pattern:

3 : 4 POLYRHYTHM:

3 : 2 POLYRHYTHM:

5 : 4 POLYRHYTHM:

4 : 3 POLYRHYTHM:

We shall visit polyrhythms again later, but now we're going back to the snare displacements that involved moving around the backbeats. As with all the groups of exercises throughout this book, try playing them individually first, and then play through the whole lot from top to bottom consecutively. Finally, make yourself a cup of tea and relax. So, there are some full exercises, this time with various kick patterns and starting with a fixed backbeat of "2":

Now then, now then! (Then now.) We're starting to feel like we're getting somewhere, surely? And no, I didn't call you "Shirley!"

After playing those beats with a fixed backbeat of "2," it would only seem right to do the exact same thing with a fixed backbeat of "4." Tally ho! Here we go:

I can read your mind and sense that you thought those were all relatively easy. Am I right? No need to answer that because I already knew. Anyhow, regardless of what you thought, we're now going to tackle some combination exercises. It's pretty much a case of "Anything goes" at this point. After keeping things somewhat grounded by adhering to at least one regular backbeat, we're just going to go ahead and stir up a little insanity here:

To finish off this look at straight eighth note beats, we're going to change the amount of said eighth note counts in a given measure. Yes, that's right folks - we're looking into alternative time signatures! Don't give me any excuses, I know you can all count because of "The Count"! (Let's face facts - he was better than Big Bird and his moral advice or Grover and his psychotic tendencies. And don't even get me started on Oscar.)

Just in case you need it, let's have a quick brush up on how time signatures work. There are two numbers at the beginning of a section of music, one being on top of the other. The upper number tells you the amount of counts (or beats) in a bar and the bottom number indicates what note value each count (or beat) is worth. So, if the bottom number is a "4," read that as a quarter note; if the bottom number is an "8," read that as an eighth note, and so on. (For reference, please visit the "In Referendum" section at the back of this book.) It's fairly easy to pick up as you go along. The beauty of differing time signatures is that it almost feels like it's your own little secret, and no one outside of the band is in on it. Well, let's face it - you can probably include the singer with them also.

Up until now, we've been using a 4/4 time signature, which is also known as "Common Time." Under this framework, we are grouping our rhythms into four beats per measure. Keeping quarter notes as the base counts for now, we will begin to explore switching out the top number and therefore changing the amount of counts in a bar. For starters, here is a look at some eighth note beats under a 3/4 time signature:

Fabulous! Next up, we will be looking at a 5/4 time signature. This is where things get a bit weird (in a Salvador Dali kind of way). You won't find a whole lot of songs that use this counting framework, so it's a good one. The most famous one that you should all know, however, is called … ummm … I can't remember. Bugger! Whatever it was, let's now Take Five:

Are you all still present? Wonderful. Thought I might be losing you there for a second …
Let's now conclude this chapter with a gander at the 7/4 time signature. While slightly more
popular than the 5/4 (though still pretty rare), we shall attempt to make life very, very difficult
for you all the same:

Chapter Three: Where Did You Say You Wanted These?

Okey dokey, the time is now upon us to explore the good old "off-beat." So far, we've been synchronizing our snares and kicks with our hi-hats, because that is a good manner in which to begin our crazy journey into the land of Topsy Turvy. Just as you begin to feel all cozy and settled in, we pull the rug out from beneath your feet.

However, before throwing you under the (double decker) bus, it would be a good idea to have a quick shufty at "check patterns." These beauties are all variations on a group of sixteenth notes, with different pieces missing. It's important to be familiar with all of the check patterns because they are a large part of the overall language of drumming. If you can learn them off-by-heart, you are well on your way to becoming a tip-top, savvy sight reader.

To understand these rhythms, let's look at them within the context of a sixteenth note framework: 1 e & a | 2 e & a | 3 e & a | 4 e & a. Now, when counting out those sixteenth notes in full, it's just simply a case of when to hit and when not to. Sometimes, we strike three of those counts, sometimes two, and sometimes only one. Either way, always count all of them.

So then, here are those check patterns, following a group of individual sixteenth note counts (not worrying about straight quarter notes or eighth notes):

Before beginning some exercises, it would be exquisite if we all warmed up. The best way to do this is to grab a hot cup of English Breakfast and get those juices flowing (quite literally, if you drink it half as much as me)! After that, let's work on some sixteenth note fragments and get a decent feel for hitting the snares and kicks "off" the beat. Make sure that your hi-hats remain nice and even while performing these warm ups:

Fantastic! So then, to move ourselves onwards and upwards, we are going to revisit the exercises we played back in Chapter Two, but this time we'll drop some check patterns into the mix. There's nothing like progress, my dear drumming friends!

Here are some eighth note beats with a fixed backbeat of "2," incorporating check patterns:

How are you feeling? If the answer relates to tumble dryers or washing machines, then good for you! Your head is supposed to be in a spin right about now because you are throwing your limbs around in places where they usually don't go. And that is a good thing.

Now, pull it all together again because we are doing the same with a solid "4" backbeat:

Because you are enjoying these so much, we're going to look at some additional beats that use check patterns. These exercises can also be found in *The Teacher and Student Method Drum Set Studies: Exercise Book Two.* (I've heard great things about that book, I wonder who wrote it?)

Right then, this is yer first lot:

We are just spoiling you right now, aren't we? And no, I don't have any Ferrero Rocher on me ...

Here are more eighth note beats that incorporate check patterns. You may also find these exercises available on our website, **teacherandstudentbooks.com**, in the "Free Bonus Exercises" section, along with other additional materials from our method series:

"You spin me right round. Baby, right round. Like a record spinning right round."

Are we trying to reinvent the wheel here? Not really, but we may feel like one right now! Trust me, though. We need to be kept on our toes every now and again (it's good for the calf muscles, after all). Anyhow, let's now lob some check patterns into these combination beats:

You are probably wondering if anyone actually plays these kinds of beats in music. The answer, of course, is "yes!" Ever since the early 90's (a long time ago, in a galaxy far, far away), electronic music has been gaining popularity, especially in the clubs. No, no, we are not talking about your local cricket club or bingo hall, but the places where people dance like (spasmodic) robots, the nightclubs!

Of course, pretty much all of modern dance music is programmed on a computer by individuals who may never have even picked up an instrument. However, because of their lack of music "education" and little knowledge of the conventional ways of doing things, some very interesting things have been happening. These "Beatmakers" will take the programming of a beat, or even a recorded sample, and then chop it up and stitch it back together again (hence the term "breakbeat"). Sometimes, the rhythm and patterns sound a bit "off" to the regular listener, but that is the whole point. The idea is to create a new sound that is lively and frenetic that still follows (for the most part) a 4/4 time signature pattern, even though the backbeat is constantly thrown around. It's an exciting new way of creating beats. Some of these forms of electronic music, also know as "club" or "dance," have become increasingly popular in the underground scene, particularly the likes of jungle, drum 'n' bass, garage, acid house, techno, and more recently, dubstep.

That's all well and good, but where does that leave us "real" drummers? Well, certain "Stickmen" have been bringing these wild creations to the kit. Check out Johnny Rabb, JoJo Mayer, Tony Verderosa, Ydna Murd, Zach Dazinger, and even the legendary Steve Smith (who likes to dabble). The idea is to play it extremely fast and loose, which is a lot of fun for the player. Crikey, it's even considered to be a workout, if you play it often enough! Not to mention, a good exercise for the brain.

We're going to revisit these breakbeats again later on, but now it's time to switch things up a little. Looking back at our Latin grooves, it's fun to take an existing beat and give it the makeover treatment (with no lipstick or eyeliner involved). All will be revealed on the next page (no peeking, now). But, before we do that, let's take a butchers at a new one, which is a variation of the Afro-Cuban "samba" rhythm:

Are you curious? I hope so. And now for the big reveal ... those aforementioned Latin beats will be made over with ... some check patterns! As I said earlier, we're trying to look at things a little differently here, so what better than to take some "traditional" beats and modernize them? Well, regardless of how that makes you feel, I've gone and bleeding well done it anyway ...

The cool thing here is the coming together of two different genres: Latin and club music. This is the kind of original thinking you want to be exploring, if you want to be remembered in the years to come. Anyhow, let's now close out this chapter with those beats, as promised:

2 / 3 SON CLAVE:

2 / 3 RUMBA CLAVE:

2 / 3 BOSSA NOVA CLAVE:

2 / 3 SAMBA CLAVE:

Chapter Four: Is It Really As Easy As 1, 2, 3?

Triplets! No, I'm not talking about your deepest and darkest fantasies here because it's time to look at groups of three, in musical terms, of course. For those of you who have been living under a rock (not to mention, have probably been playing too much rock), here is a quick look at how we count a straight eighth note triplet beat:

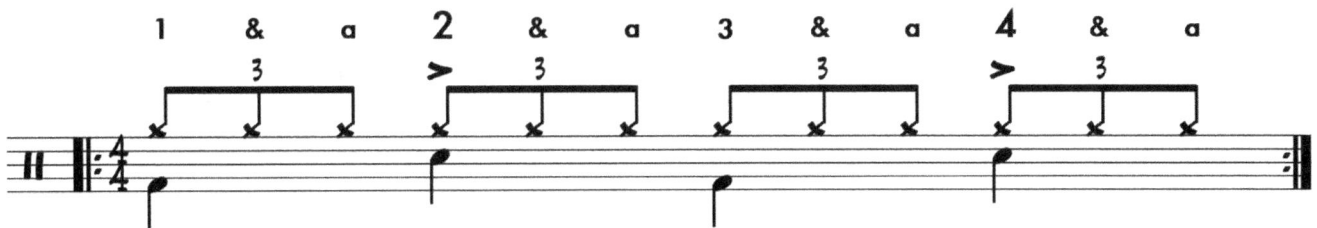

Some of you may count these as "one tri- plet | two tri- plet | three tri- plet | four tri- plet," which is also fine. I'm not going to hold it against you! (I'm a pacifist, remember?) Whatever you decide, the most important factor is to really feel that count of three, which takes some getting used to if you don't play triplets on a regular basis.

Just like with our sixteenth notes, triplets also have their own set of check patterns. Let us, then, have a quick scan at those, within the context of a single group of eighth note triplets:

Alrighty, then! Just like with our regular eight note beats, we shall start you off gently. Why? Because we believe that breathing is good, so it's nice to allow ourselves the space to do so. It's even better when accompanied with a nice cup of Assam. All done? Okay, let's play some eighth note triplet beats with a fixed backbeat of "2":

How is the power of three treating thee so far? Smiling with frustration yet? Grinning through gritted teeth? As they say, "No pain no gain!" (Just remember that the next time you have to lug your entire drum set up two flights of stairs.) Anyhow, back to the present, and you know the score ... more eighth note triplet beats, now with a consistent backbeat of "4":

Chocks away! I just know that you are enjoying these triplets, so we're going to give you some more. All you can do is continue to "tri" your best. Geddit? Sure, we're all drummers here, so we appreciate the odd bad joke, or twenty. And, let's face it - we have to have a good sense of humor, when guitars are tuning up for half a gig. Never mind, here are some triplet combos:

Now that straight eighth note triplets have been covered, let's turn our attention again to off-beats. Sixteenth note triplets (sextuplets) will give us quite a few possible combinations over a recurring pattern of six, which means that things can quite easily get a bit messy, especially when writing things down. Our note values (how long we count when we see a certain note or rhythm) haven't changed from our regular sixteenth notes, but we now have an extra two sixteenth notes to cover with each individual beat of the bar. If all of this is translating to something like "h@d*ui dbb;v xd#csx%jy ie=nd!obe fv ..." I'm sorry. As always, my friendly advice would be to sit down with a soothing cuppa and drink until the powers-that-be bestow their wisdom upon you. It usually works for me!

So, we're not going to look at any new check patterns (yay) because the ones that we learned back in Chapter Three will also work here. It's just important to remember that regarding our new counting framework of six sixteenth note triplets, a regular quarter note will cover four of those counts; a dotted eighth note will cover three; a regular eighth note will cover two; and a sixteenth note will cover one. Got that? Fantabulous!

If you're still confused, it's best just to look through the exercises and simply hit stuff either with the hi-hat, or in-between the hi-hats, while maintaining a steady beat throughout. Then leave all of that other nonsense at the door or with us nerds that have nothing better to do with our "time."

However, we're still going to get you all in shape and ready for the beach by giving you some warm up exercises. Try playing these individually, then from start to finish:

Dapper! See, it's really not all that bad, is it?

Well, you guys all know the drill by now (a statement you never want to hear when visiting the dentist). Yes, we shall be recapping our eighth note triplet beats, but slotting in some sixteenth note triplet check patterns. First up, a consistent backbeat of "2":

Feeling "beat," yet? But, of course not. You're just getting started here, and we have many more triplet beats on the road ahead.

So, dust off your headlights, grab your driving gloves, and pour your hot tea into a Thermos. Here, then, are more eighth note triplet beats with check patterns, locking on the "4":

"Easy peasy, pudding and pie." That's what my mum used to say to me, when she saw steam blowing out of my ears. It's only now that I've realized how much she liked to tell fibs just to get me to be a more mellow fellow. Tsk!

Brace yourselves, dear readers, because here is the first group of combination exercises:

It's now time to finish off this chapter with a "Bang!" We don't want you to be left wanting more, like little Oliver Twist. And I am no Scrooge, so we can happily oblige ...

Speaking of "twists," for this last group of exercises, there should be a little bit more of that this time. Thom Yorke, of Radiohead, loves to dance to these fine combination beats. Enjoy:

Chapter Five: Just Who Is This "Lynn" Character, And What About Her Ear?

No, no, no ... that's *Linear*, not "Lynn's ear!" Linear beats and exercises are all about using our limbs (not Lynn's) one at a time, and never synchronizing them together. In other words, we're going to be doing this all *one thing at a time*.

Sounds simple, right? Sorry to burst your bubble here, but it's not as hunky dory as you might think because we will be exploring some full-on "Drum Twisters" later on. However, let's break things down first. You've probably all played an eighth note linear beat at some point, similar to the following:

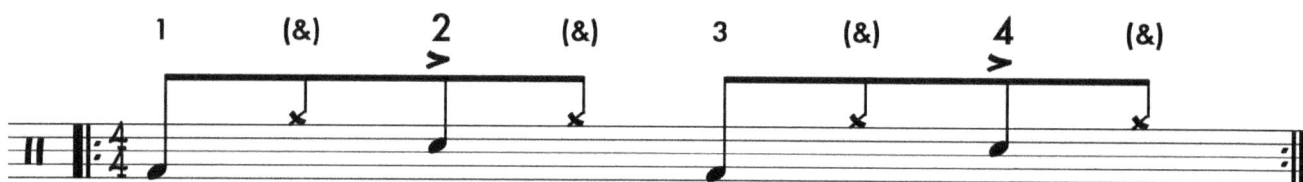

As you can see, we follow a steady eighth note counting pattern, but only hit one thing for each individual count. This is how we'll be doing things at the start, but of course (in true Drum Twisters fashion) with the beats all moved around. And, yes ... upside down!

Slow down now, let's do some simple linear warm ups first. These single eighth note exercises should be played with the regular hands and feet you use when playing a beat:

Brilliant! We should be in some kind of position to try out some beats now.

This time around, we're just going to throw some mixed exercises your way. There are varying backbeats here, so keep your eyes peeled and your senses alert. If you don't normally use a metronome (a popular garden ornament that lives in the city), then now would be the time:

This is the kind of thing that will put hairs on your chest, right? Which is good news, if you're a little short on top and need some extra hair to compensate! My dad once explained to me why some people were bald, and I think he blamed it on a poor chap named Al O' Peshia?

Regardless, we're going to launch straight into some combination beats now:

Now, onto sixteenth note linear beats. These chaps will work the same way as the eighth notes, but we've got some extra ground to cover for each count (or beat). Please note that not all of the snares are accented this time, just the ones that make up our actual backbeats.

Let's revisit our first group of eighth note linear beats, but give them a sixteenth note pattern:

Hold on to your horses because things are about to get a little bumpy here! (Mexicans can alternatively hold on to their burro, and Americans can hold on to their ass.)

We're now going to be using *all* of our limbs in a four-way coordination. Notice that we are now incorporating the ride cymbal and hi-hat pedal. Before we enter the Grand National, however, let's take some time to warm up with the following exercises:

Splendid! Alternatively, you can use a double kick pedal and have both feet playing kick on these four-way exercises. Another option is to play the hi-hat instead of the ride so that when you place your foot on the pedal, it will create some open and closed hi-hats. Whatever floats your boat. Here are some full sixteenth note linear beats, this time utilizing every limb:

We have giveth, and now we shall taketh away! Yes, that's right folks. We are removing some of the sixteenth notes by using check patterns with our linear beats. Things may seem a bit "choppy" at first when playing these because the rhythms are all over the place (please revert back to our "spasmodic robot" reference). Regardless, we shall soldier on, fixing on the "2":

What's all this about then? You know what's going to happen next? Well, that may be so, but now it's time to climb off your high horse (or burro, etc.) and start walking the walk. Yes, we're going to be playing some more beats here, genius! So then, give yourselves a pat on the back and tackle some more linear beats with check patterns, using a locked backbeat of "4":

It's a rush to the finish line ... not really. We're going to conclude this chapter by bringing back all four of our limbs. (Stop groaning at the back there.) So, it may feel more like a limp, or perhaps even a silly walk. Whatever style you may be trundling along with (off our beat(en) path, of course), just remember not to curse at the Man in the sky. It's not His fault for these:

Chapter Six: Can I Please Get My Groove Back On, Baby?

Yes! Now that we've messed around with some linear exercises, it's time to return to a more flowing way of doing things. In this chapter, we're going to look at some additional beats from around the world, but this time with differing hi-hat patterns.

Let us first continue with our Afro-Cuban and Latin beats. So far, things have been flowing in a steady, eighth note pattern. However, many world beats have variations with the rhythm hand which can be played on the hi-hats, ride, and even the cowbell (more of that, please, Gene Frenkle).

Returning to our samba beat, we shall now play it with a more traditional rhythm pattern on the top. Practice this sequence on the ride cymbal until you can do it in your sleep:

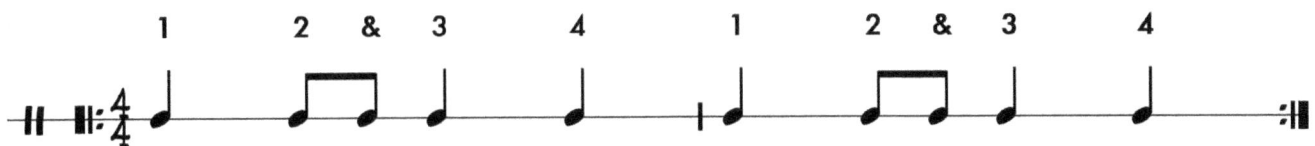

Okay, now that that's sorted, it's time to bring in the beat section (our snares and kick). We've played this before, back at the end of Chapter Three, but now we're going to insert some hi-hat pedal on beats "2" and "4" of the bar. The accents on a traditional samba are not set in stone, so don't feel like you are stuck with what the following example demonstrates; I just decided on the snare hits that align with the ride to offer some continuity here. Anyhow, let's add some pico de gallo to garnish and put it all together for our traditional samba:

Pip pip, my dear drummers! Aren't we feeling all exotic? The world (music) is now your oyster, but you have to come out of your shell, first! (That was a pearl of a joke, right there.)

Just a little sidenote: It's important to mention that most of the time, Latin beats use a cross stick instead of a snare, so please feel free to use those if you want to try the more formal approach. However, if you prefer the contemporary version that says "DRUMS" rather than just "drums," please stick with those snares. Hmmm, but rimshots might be a stretch!

Before we try to take on, ahem, the world, let's have a look at some more Afro-Cuban patterns to be played with the rhythm hand. Here are six more to get you in the mood:

Hey hombre! Now that we're getting a feel for this, let's add in some beats that compliment those rhythmic patterns. Latin is a lot like jazz in that we have the opportunity to "freestyle" with beats, so long as it compliments the ostinato feet, clave, or rhythm hand. Here, then, are some example beats (also including ghost notes), using the rhythms from the previous page:

MAMBO (WITH COWBELL):

CASCARA (WITH CROSS STICK):

MOZAMBIQUE (WITH CROSS STICK):

SONGO:

BOMBA:

CONGA:

Viva! Saúde! Hope you enjoyed this brief look at Latin American beats. If you would like to play more, check out *Afro-Cuban Rhythms for Drumset* by Frank Malabe and Bob Weiner.

We're going to turn our attention now to jazz. Nice! Primarily, jazz music heeds to a "swing" rhythm, using a repeated hand sequence of a quarter note followed by a swing triplet. Here is a quick lookie at how that plays out on the ride cymbal:

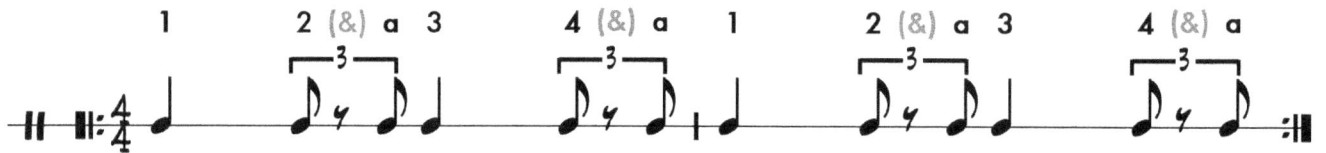

Underneath our swing rhythm, we usually play combinations of quarter notes and triplets, such as back in Chapter Four. Freeform (also know simply as "free") is a much more improvised and frenetic version of jazz, that often moves backbeats all over the place. So that is the direction we will be taking for now, although approached in a structured and intentional manner. Plus, of course, putting our own unique (drum) twist on things!

Before messing things up, let's really get that swing rhythm down first by warming up with some straight jazz swing beats. See that our backbeats are accentuated with a hi-hat pedal:

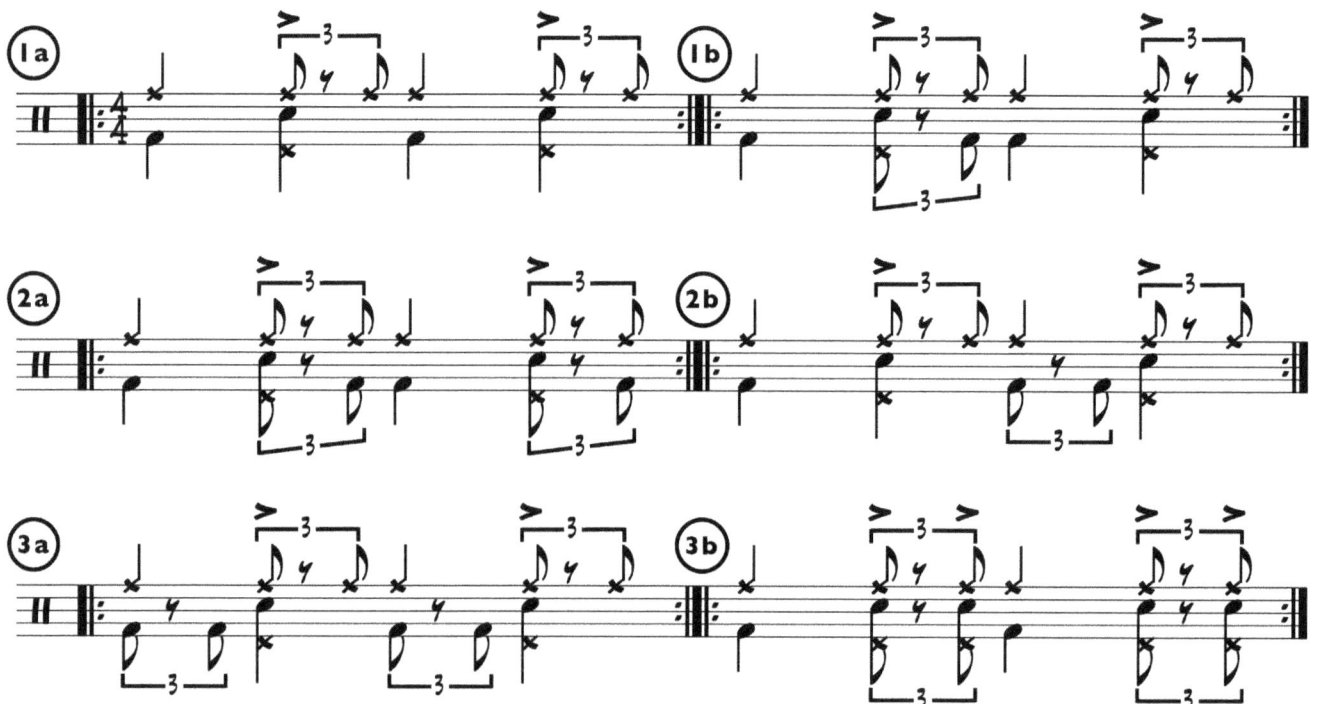

Cooooooool, man. Now that you're feeling like a "cat," let's do those swing beats again, but this time with the backbeats moved around:

Grooooooovy, baby. Time now to insert some regular eighth note triplet patterns into the mix:

Thought we were done with those? Not so fast, daddy-o! There's still some bonus exercises lying around to get the blood pumping. Time, though, to add in a little "heat."

We're going to play more of these swing beats with eighth note triplets, but this time "jive" with some ghost notes. Well, you did ask for something groovy, so no blowing your top:

Let's now "jump" on some sixteenth note triplets. This is where our version of free jazz starts to get a little warped! Before you go ahead and "screw the pooch," just be aware that I'm easing you in gently. So, you can save the real "clinkers" for the next page instead.

Right then, let's take those last beats to the next level. Evolution is a wonderful thing:

Swingin'! Now then, it's time to revisit some old friends of ours. For this next group of exercises, we're going to call upon some random beats from the end of Chapter Four. You know, the ones that left you with a bald patch up top? Yes, *those* ones!

Let's not get caught up on swings and roundabouts now, but "bust it" on these instead:

In conclusion, it's safe to say that jazz is a very sophisticated beast, particularly the freeform style of playing. Of course, we offered our own interpretation here because really this kind of playing is freestyled and not preconceived. It's also really difficult to notate this stuff and get you "hip" to the feel, especially regarding the subtleties in the dynamics.

Because of its improvisational qualities, there isn't really a transcription book I can recommend for free jazz itself, so the next best thing to do is check out *Advanced Techniques for the Modern Drummer* by Jim Chapin for an extensive look at general swing beats. You can then explore and expand the possibilities from there if you really want to (be) "fly."

Jazz requires much listening to be understood. Some free jazz artists that you should check out are John Coltrane, Pharaoh Sanders, Cecil Taylor, Jackie McLean, the Jimmy Giuffre Trio, Sun Ra, and of course, Chick Corea. Over the decades, jazz has morphed itself into other styles and genres, and we generally know this as "jazz fusion," or simply "fusion" (Miles Davis, Herbie Hancock, Ray Charles). Beyond that, jazz has further moved into the mainstream with styles known as "jazz rock" (Van Morrison, Caravan, Chicago); "jam bands" (Grateful Dead, Traffic, Santana); and "progressive rock" (Frank Zappa, Jethro Tull, Pink Floyd).

Another variation of standard jazz that is extremely popular, is our good old friend the "blues." Some may argue that the blues is directly responsible for rock 'n' roll, because it really helped to straighten out jazz and make it more accessible. Whatever you may think, the most common form of blues (rhythmically) is known as the "shuffle," which is quite simply a repeating pattern of swing triplets, like so:

Feel free to revisit our swing beats in this chapter, and try them with a shuffle rhythm on top instead. Just so you know, shuffles are also popular in country music. Anyhow, once you are done with that, y'all come on back now, ya hear?

Whatever style of music is considered to be your "bag," you can be sure that there is some form of jazz in there somewhere. So, "dig it" and then "break it down!"

If you're "solid" with that, then let's end this chapter and "split" for now.

Chapter Seven: Oh, So This Is What They Mean By A "Drum Off"?

Ummm, no, not quite! What we will be looking at now is check patterns, but this time played on the hi-hat. We explored this to some degree in our previous chapter, but now we're getting a lot more varied. The possibilities here are truly endless, but I have a home to get back to, so we're only going so far with it. And besides, it's nearly time for my supper!

Beginning with our sixteenth note check patterns, we'll be exploring our breakbeats again. For the first time in this book, some of our backbeats (accents) will be without a hi-hat. That's just the way the cookie crumbles, so don't cry over spilled milk. Yum, milk and cookies ...

Before we get cracking, we should first do some warm ups. If you recall the check pattern counts from the beginning of Chapter Three, we're now going to play those with a simple beat underneath. But beware because darkness lies around the corner:

Next, we will look at all of those sixteenth note hi-hat check patterns individually, but with varying breakbeats underneath. Right, here is yer first lot:

Indeedy, I think you're getting the (blurred) picture now. Let's not hesitate, but move swiftly along to our next hi-hat check pattern. Feel free to "ghost" all off-beat snares from here on:

Bravo! Have you also noticed that we now have backbeats on the "e" and the "a" in regards to our counts? But, of course you did. Okay then, feast your eyes on these:

Right on, my partners in crime! Noise pollution intrusion is what we do best. Having said that, let's do some more misdemeanors and paint the town red:

Okay, that's the check patterns done with three hits in them, so now it's on to the twos. Please tread carefully here because Admiral Ackbar warned us of a trap ahead:

Jolly good! Well, it sure beats skiing, doesn't it? Not sure why anyone would risk life and limb(s) doing that. It's a slippery slope, I tell you … kind of like these:

Howzat? Like a "storm in a teacup," you say? Well, I'm not so sure about a storm, but I could sure do with a tantalizing brew of Ceylon right about now. Put the kettle on and drink to this:

Onto the final pattern of two hi-hats, and it's a doozy. But, like all good things in life, you've got to take the bull by the horns (though never in a china shop). Smashing! Here we go:

Lovely jubbly! In our countdown so far we've done three hits, then two, and now we're down to our single hi-hat check pattern strikes. Right, give me an "e" please, Bob:

Has the breakbeat broken you or beaten you, yet? If so, best take a break, as you're feeling beat. Now then, break back into your stride and don't beat yourself up with these:

Coolio! Now, before moving onto triplets again, we're going to finish up these breakbeats with a thorough look at the straight eighth note "off-beat" pattern (hi-hats on the "&" only). This is the rhythm you hear most when a hi-hat is irregular, which is especially popular with reggae and some bolder forms of electronic music. Let's have some fun, then, with these little devils, including some ghost notes on the off-beat snares. Spooky, indeed:

Chipper! We shall turn our attention now to triplet check patterns on the hi-hat. If you refer back to the beginning of Chapter Four, here are the remainders which are left unchallenged:

Those ghosts haven't gone away! Who ya gonna call? That's right, the "Beatbusters" for these:

Right then, just two more hi-hat triplet check patterns to go! We've looked at the rhythms with two hits, so now we're down to the ones. Have a squizzy at these little delights:

And for the curtain call to this chapter, take a bow but don't bow out on these curiosities:

Chapter Eight: You Must Be Bloody Joking, Right?

I wish that I was, my fellow drummers, but it's time to start the winding down process with some final hair-pulling exercises, to extend out your bald patch. For this last chapter looking at beats, we're going to jumble everything together that we have learned thus far, sort of like a bring & buy sale but trading small pieces of our sanity instead of Aunt Hilda's jam tarts. Before we do that, however, let's take a meander back to our polyrhythms. Since our initial visit, we've been working extensively with sixteenth notes and off-beats, which can also be incorporated into our polyrhythmic counting frameworks.

As an example, we will look again at our 3:4 bossa nova polyrhythm from Chapter Two, but this time using sixteenth note counts for our pattern of three on top:

Yes, I know what you're thinking ... how do Chinese people perform the dance to the YMCA song? You also may be murmuring about how we now have off-beats that are considered as backbeats (accents). It happens, folks! We can really enhance our peculiar and off-putting rhythms by hammering home those hits that are nowhere near where they should be (a bit like me). You know, just to be all awkward, like.

Of course, our sixteenth note polyrhythmic patterns can also be used to count our kick drum. This leaves us with many possible combinations, more than we can shake a stick at, even (quite literally, being drummers). So, we're just going to dip a single hand into the cookie jar here, and then not take too big a slice of the pie ...

Am I the only one here that really fancies something sweet right now?

Because we want to cram in as many exercises as we can, there will no longer be any number counts visible for our polyrhythms. You're just going to have to assume we know what we are talking about here (dangerous, I know)! Okay, here's our first lot, using sixteenth notes for the number counts and incorporating some hi-hat check patterns:

Brill! Are we having fun counting two things at the same time? It's a bit like juggling, only with drum components instead of balls or pins. Wait ... I don't mean that literally, so please put down your hi-hat stand! Now then, we're going to look at one more group of exercises using polyrhythms, but this time following a sixteenth note triplet framework:

Are you fighting the frustration? I hope so because we've all got a little hair still remaining on our heads. Time to ease back on the throttle now (while still letting the wind sail through said hair), and return to our good old friends, la breakbeats! Let us now attempt to play them using a variety of different time signatures, starting with another look at 3/4 and mixing up the hi-hat patterns. As Dracula famously bespoke, "Once bitten, forever smitten:"

TA-DA! Now, here are more delights, but using a triplet framework:

Now, with slightly less hair up top but significantly more love in our hearts, we shall continue on with these sheer pleasures. Where to go now? Five, you say? (I'm assuming that by raising your hand, you are putting five fingers up and not begging me to stop.) Well, you've all asked, and now you shall receive ... here are more breakbeats with varying hi-hat patterns, this time following a 5/4 time signature:

And then there was the group of threes:

Seeing as things are beginning to get a little cramped within our exercises, we're going to un-snug the bug in a rug. (Really, what was so comforting about that in the first place, anyway?) So, the following exercises will be stretched across the whole line and will be using various time signatures. Grab your tea and a scone before we tackle these blighters in 7/4:

Wicked! Now, let's try out some shenanigans using a 9/4 time signature:

Anyone up for elevenses?

Time to dial back now and look at time a little differently. I suppose you could say that I am a Time Lord. (Who? Yes, but I'm no Doctor.) So, we're going to be using time signatures with eight as our bottom number. This doesn't affect how we read or interpret these beats, just how we count them and how the notes are grouped together. With that said, why don't we try and hit it for a six, which will feel familiar as it's almost the same as our 3/4 time signature:

And now let's triple our luck here:

Getting close to the end of the tunnel now, dear readers. It's been quite a ride (or hi-hat) with these little beats of ours. Just keep moving towards that light, unless it's the "430762" from London to Bristol. However, let us remain in the darkness just a little longer while tackling these beats in 10/8. We're now going to add some sixteenth triplets to the hi-hat patterns:

How's about some lucky thirteen?

Not quite "sweet sixteen," but seventeen will do:

Well, it's been a long journey full of blood, sweat and tears (and lots of tea). We're reaching our final destination now with our beat-making and general bad behavior. All of us are all bald, haggard, beaten senseless, and left out for the neighborhood cats, but we've done it (mostly) with smiles upon our faces. When you go down with that sinking ship, though, legend has it that you're supposed to play on. Here, then, is our final curtain call, so remember to grin like the Cheshire Cat as you experience that drowning feeling henceforth:

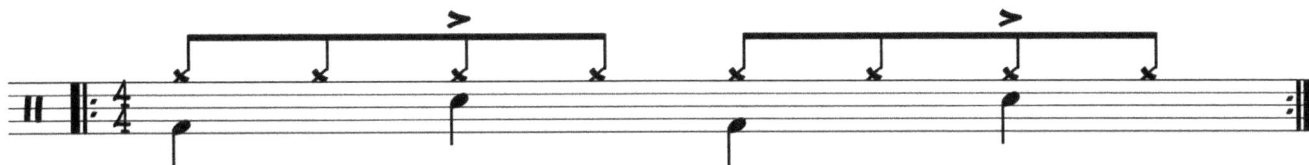

Wait … what? All joking aside, this final beat is one of the most important that you will ever play. It is also one of the most challenging because it is difficult to call your own.

When you next perform with your band or musical ensemble, remember that your passion, skill, temperament, personality, and creativity, should be poured into EVERYTHING that you do, not just the parts that you find the most thrilling. We've covered all kinds of complexities in this book, but we're now going full circle and ending up right where we began. Well, we do like to be challenged by round things, don't we?

Playing the drums isn't only about showing off what you have accomplished on a technical level, it's also about placing yourself into those notes. This is what will make you stand out as a drummer and ensure that people will notice your own unique style and persona. So, go ahead and try the above beat again. See how you can play it differently from how everyone else would play it. Then, apply that same mindset to everything else that you play from now on (including, maybe, another run through this book).

Sometimes, the most challenging things are also the most straightforward. "The devil is in the details," as they say, so be a little devil and show us all what YOU'VE got.

And never forget to smile, because frustration sure is fun.

Cheerio for now …

Chapter Nine: Are You Ever Going To "Fill" This Hole In My Heart?

This book, so far, has been all about playing beats, which is good because that is what we drummers do most of the time, when we're not propping up a bar (measure) somewhere. But now that we are beat(en) senseless, it's time to look at some fill ideas. Seeing as we are all about the twisting of the drums (or screw), we're going to look at ways to incorporate all of our limbs into fills, as well as finding ways to get them all jumbled up. That's right, ladies and gents, it's time to start using our "Drum Twisters" in a much more literal sense!

However, let's begin our look at fills by breaking things down and continuing on with our method of doing the conventional in an unconventional way. (I always wondered why the unconventional never decided to all get together somewhere … they could call it the "Unconventional Against Convention Convention.") Anyhow, we should really be focusing our attention on moving forward, so to speak. As a wheel (on the bus) goes round and round, we can start by looking at some patterns that move around the kit in a circular fashion. (Note: our left-handed friends will have to do everything back-to-front from here on.)

Beginning with a single stroke roll and some straight sixteenth note patterns on the snare, we will first substitute the beat counts (1, 2, 3 & 4, in this case) with a clockwise movement around the toms, and then kick:

Now, as with all of these initial fills, you should also sequence the toms and kick in the other direction, in a counterclockwise movement like this:

I'm sure that you are getting the idea, in a roundabout sort of way (but without those swings, this time). Now then, we shall have a dekko at those remaining counts, and don't forget to play these counterclockwise as well:

So, you probably noticed that when you were hitting the toms with your left stick, you had to move one arm over the other. This is called a "crossover," and although it's something we do very often while playing beats with the hi-hat (unless you use open sticking), it's something we rarely do while playing around with the rest of the kit.

If you've ever watched a drumline perform, you will have noticed some fellas (or bellas) carrying around a whole collection of drums in front of them. These are commonly known as "quads" or "tenors" and can be anywhere from 4-6 drums arranged in a semicircle. Now then, these talented drummers quite often have to perform using crossovers. It seems only fair that we should be getting in on that action as well ...

Before we start digging in and tying ourselves in knots, it's important to think about our technique. Crossovers work best when our shoulders are poised high (imagine a tennis ball is under both armpits), but movement is limited to positioning the arms only, and not being used as part of the actual stroke. Our elbows should be relaxed and as low as possible, so that the forearms will have more room to maneuver over each other without clashing. (If you sit far away from your kit, it might be a good idea to move in closer.) Finally, keep your wrists nice and loose, and make sure that they both have full movement at all times. Try to avoid having one hand directly above the other when striking the drums.

Let us, then, play around with some warmups next so that we can better get the individual crossovers down (right-over-left and left-over-right). Here are some straightforward patterns where one hand remains stationary while the other circles around the kit in a clockwise motion. Please note that a stick performing a crossover (above the other) is written in italics:

Awesome sauce! Now, we can look into switching up our crossovers so that we are using both in a single exercise. To do this, we are going to follow a different sticking pattern, as well as moving around the kit in both directions:

Speaking of alternate stickings, how's about toying with some regular paradiddle patterns using single crossovers:

And just like before, we can ignite that fire from deep within by trying out some paradiddles using both crossover patterns:

Okay then, now that the fun and games are over, let's piece together some exercises. We've messed around with the basic paradiddles, so that leaves us with these other variations. The left-over-right patterns are on the left, and the right-over-left patterns are on the right ... and that leaves nothing left, right? Also, we're going to keep the crossover hand stationary this time while the lower hand moves around the kit (warning, severe cramping ahead):

REVERSE PARADIDDLES:

INWARD PARADIDDLES:

OUTWARD PARADIDDLES:

So then, are your wrists and hands black and blue yet? Have you cracked your knuckles once or twice with your sticks? Once again, it's about "No pain, no gain." That just doesn't seem right when you are failing to jump over hurdles because it hurts AND you lose your ground. Hmmm, am I talking literally or metaphorically here? I guess that depends on whether or not you like to jump onto the drum riser. I've had some fun experiences doing that myself, and there's nothing like head-butting a crash cymbal in such a profound and meaningful way ...

Yes, yes, I know, the smartypants in you can tell what will happen next. Here, then, are our paradiddle variants, but this time using both crossovers in a single exercise:

REVERSE PARADIDDLE:

INWARD PARADIDDLE:

OUTWARD PARADIDDLE:

What's that you say, there's more paradiddles out there? Okay, okay, keep your hair on ... Wait, never mind, we lost all of our hair back in Chapter Eight!

Anyway, I concede; here are the triplet variations of our paradiddle chums. The first one is right-over-left, the second is left-over-right, and the last one uses both in a crossover switch. Make sure to wash these down with a nice Darjeeling afterwards:

PARADIDDLE-DIDDLE (RIGHT LEADING):

PARADIDDLE-DIDDLE (LEFT LEADING):

DOUBLE PARADIDDLE:

Since that is all done and dusted (unlike my porch), where to next? That's right, the feets!

We should probably warm up first, so here's a look at some straight (no crossover) two-way linear patterns between our hands and feet, sticking with our main paradiddles first:

PARADIDDLES:

1a (R) L (R) (R) L (R) L L   **1b** R (L) R R (L) R (L) (L)

REVERSE PARADIDDLES:

2a (R) (R) L (R) L L (R) L   **2b** R R (L) R (L) (L) R (L)

INWARD PARADIDDLES:

3a (R) L L (R) L (R) (R) L   **3b** R (L) (L) R (L) R R (L)

OUTWARD PARADIDDLES:

4a (R) L (R) L L (R) L (R)   **4b** R (L) R (L) (L) R (L) R

So so-so (said the so-and-so). I so-pose we will bring those triplet paradiddles to the mix:

PARADIDDLE-DIDDLES (RIGHT LEADING):

1a (R) L (R) (R) L L (R) L (R) (R) L L   **1b** R (L) R R (L) (L) R (L) R R (L) (L)

PARADIDDLE-DIDDLES (LEFT LEADING):

2a L (R) L L (R) (R) L (R) L L (R) (R)   **2b** (L) R (L) (L) R R (L) R (L) (L) R R

DOUBLE PARADIDDLES:

3a (R) L (R) L (R) (R) L (R) L (R) (L) (L)   **3b** R (L) R (L) R R (L) R (L) (R) (L) (L)

Sweet! We're going to put this all together now and perform some full (four-way) linear fills incorporating paradiddle patterns. These exercises are tackled first using open sticking on the left, and then with crossovers on the right. What are you getting all cross over? Fretting is for guitarists only. Just look cool, even though you're hurting inside. As the great Michael Caine once said, "Be like a duck. Calm on the surface, but paddling like the dickens underneath ... "

PARADIDDLES:

REVERSE PARADIDDLES:

INWARD PARADIDDLES:

OUTWARD PARADIDDLES:

PARADIDDLE-DIDDLES (RIGHT LEADING):

PARADIDDLE-DIDDLES (LEFT LEADING):

DOUBLE PARADIDDLES:

How you diddling? I hope that you're not *para*-lyzed. Anyhow, we're getting mighty close to wrapping this whole thing up, so I just need you to stay conscious for a little while longer. If you are in need of a pick-me-up, then I've heard that Lady Grey can work her wonders. She's also not quite as bitter as her husband, the Earl of the Grey, so that's nice.

What would you like to do next? Any last requests? I'm thinking that we should continue on with some four-way linear rudiments, but maybe try out some rolls? That way, we can keep those diddles going longer, as you all love your troubles to be in doubles. Amiright?

Just make sure that you warm up your double strokes first by performing the following roll exercises on the snare only. Each double is counted as a sixteenth note but written as two thirty-second notes. You can view all of these rudiments (plus the others) for free by visiting either the PAS (Percussive Arts Society) or Vic Firth websites. Then, close your eyes and think of England while you're on top of the world with these geezers:

Well then, that's yer lot. It's time to pack up your (stick) bags and gallivant back home. That's right, ya hippies ... get off my land!!!

Ugh, all right then. I can see that you won't budge until we've finished our rolls by looking at those triplet cousins. Let's keep it all in the family, then, and show some final love for these:

SINGLE STROKE FOURS:

1a R L (R) L L R (L) R R L (R) L L R (L) R   1b R L (R) L L R (L) R R L (R) L L R (L) R

SINGLE STROKE SEVENS:

2a R L (R) L R (L) R L R (L) R L (R) L   2b R L (R) L R (L) R L R (L) R L (R) L

TRIPLE STROKE ROLLS:

3a R R (R) L L (L) R R (R) L L (L) R R (R) L L (L) R R (R) L L (L)   3b R R (R) L L (L) R R (R) L L (L) R R (R) L L (L) R R (R) L L (L)

Speaking of love, although I have nothing but the deepest feelings of it for all of you, I must now love you and leave you (tough love for a tough crowd). Just like with your favorite pair of sticks, they must be retired at some point because they are worn out, stripped to the bear minimum, and in need of a refresh. That is where we are all at ourselves, my dear drumming brothers (and sisters), and we can do no more. Well, until tomorrow, that is.

However, cheer up now, you know what they say ...

Some things in life are bad, they can really make you mad ... other things just make you swear and curse ...

Remember to keep up with your wonderful drumming, even when it frustrates you to no end. And never stop smiling because you always look on the bright side of life. That is why we drummers are the mutt's nuts, because we're a care free and jolly bunch of souls ...

Hasta la vista, baby!

All

Good

Things

Must

Come

To

Pass ...

In Referendum

This page serves as a reference to the notation and drum language that you will be using in this book. Just in case you need some guidance, here is a quick look at the type of clef we use, as well as a brief explanation of how time signatures work:

CLEF: Drums and percussion (unpitched) use the **Neutral Clef**

TIME SIGNATURE: The top number indicates the amount of beats (counts) in a measure
The bottom number indicates what note value each beat receives -
(in this case, a **quarter** note)

Next, here is a chart showing us a key of all the drum set components that we use:

HI-HAT:　　　　　　　　　　　　　　RIDE:

SNARE:　　　GHOST NOTE:　　　TOM 1:　　　TOM 2:　　　TOM 3 (FLOOR TOM):

BASS/KICK:　　　　　　　　　　　HI-HAT PEDAL:

As for the (bad) language and British slang, may I suggest you visit **urbandictionary.com** for translation. Please note that no tea leaves were harmed during the making of this book.

We have also crafted a series of books that are intended for the regular study of playing the drum set ... *The Teacher and Student Method Drum Set Studies: Exercise Books One & Two.*

www.ingramcontent.com/pod-product-compliance
Lightning Source LLC
LaVergne TN
LVHW061301060426
835509LV00016B/1672